Florida Edition

SRA Art Connections

Level K

Authors
Rosalind Ragans, Ph.D., Senior Author

Willis Bing Davis
Tina Farrell
Jane Rhoades Hudak, Ph.D.
Gloria McCoy
Bunyan Morris
Nan Yoshida

Contributing Writer
Patricia Carter

Education Division
Performing Arts Center of Los Angeles County

SRA McGraw-Hill

Columbus, Ohio

A Division of The McGraw-Hill Companies

Credits

Cover, Jack Savitsky, *Train in Coal Town*, National Museum of American Art, Smithsonian Institution, Washington, DC. Art Resource, NY. Gift of Herbert Waide Hemphill, Jr. and museum purchase made possible by Ralph Cross Johnson; **Back Cover**, top Caycee Creamer, Age 5, *Animal Parade*, middle Octavious Baker, Age 5, *Shape Quilt*, bottom Williamston Primary School, Ages 5–6, *All Through the Town*; **13**, Louvre, Paris, France; **26**, Photograph by Vic Luke; **29**, Photograph by Dirk Baker ©1996 Detroit Institute of Arts; **31**, ©1998 Estate of Grant Wood/Licensed by VAGA, New York, NY. Courtesy of the Curtis Galleries Inc., Minneapolis, MN; **44**, Photograph by Craig Schwartz; **47**, Photograph courtesy of Jerry Pinkney; **49**, Photograph courtesy of UPI/Corbis-Bettmann; **62**, Photograph by Robert Millard ©1993 courtesy of the Los Angeles Master Chorale; **65**, Photograph by David Heald. ©The Solomon R. Guggenheim Foundation, NY; **67**, Photograph by Dominique Berretty/ Black Star; **80**, Photograph courtesy of In the Heart of the Beast Puppet and Mask Theatre; **83**, Photograph courtesy of Christopher Downs; **85**, Photograph courtesy of the Museum of Fine Arts, Boston, MA; **98**, Photograph by Craig Schwartz, ©1990; **101**, Nelson-Atkins Museum of Art, including Shuttlecocks, 1994, by Coosje van Bruggen and Claes Oldenburg. Photograph by E.G. Schempf; **103**, Courtesy of Maria Martínez, ©Jerry Jacka Photography; **116**, Photograph by Neil Rickle; **119**, Photograph courtesy of Giraudon/Art Resource, NY; **140**, *Yellow Horse*, ©Douglas Mazonowicz/Gallery of Prehistoric Art; **141**, *Tutankhamen Mask (side view)*, ©Brian Brake, Photo Researchers; **142**, *Mona Lisa*, Louvre, Paris, France. Erich Lessing, Art Resource, NY; **143**, *Susan Comforting the Baby*, The Museum of Fine Arts, Houston, TX. The John A. and Audrey Jones Beck Collection; **148**, Aaron Haupt/Aaron Haupt Photography; **150**, Michael Newman/PhotoEdit; **152**, Photograph by Mark Burnet.

SRA/McGraw-Hill
*A Division of The **McGraw·Hill** Companies*

Copyright © 2001 by SRA/McGraw-Hill.

All rights reserved. Except as permitted under the United States Copyright Act, no part of this publication may be reproduced or distributed in any form or by any means, or stored in a database or retrieval system, without the prior written permission of the publisher, unless otherwise indicated.

Send all inquiries to:
SRA/McGraw-Hill
8787 Orion Place
Columbus, OH 43240-4027

Printed in the United States of America.

ISBN 0-02-684806-6

1 2 3 4 5 6 7 8 9 VHP 04 03 02 01 00

Authors

Senior Author
Dr. Rosalind Ragans, Ph. D.
Associate Professor Emerita
Georgia Southern University

Willis Bing Davis
Artist, Art Consultant
Former Art Department Chair
Central State University, Ohio

Tina Farrell
Director of Visual and
Performing Arts,
Clear Creek Independent School
District, Texas

Jane Rhoades Hudak, Ph.D.
Professor of Art
Georgia Southern University

Gloria McCoy
President,
Texas Art Education Association
K-12 Art Director, Spring Branch
Independent School District, Texas

Bunyan Morris
Art Teacher
Bulloch County School System,
Statesboro, Georgia

Nan Yoshida
Art Education Consultant,
Los Angeles, California

Contributors
ARTSOURCE Music, Dance, Theater Lessons
Education Division
Performing Arts Center of
Los Angeles
Executive Director, Music Center
Education Division–Joan Boyett
Concept Originator and
Project Director–Melinda Williams
Project Coordinator–
Susan Cambigue-Tracey
Arts Discipline Writers:
Dance–Susan Cambigue-Tracey
Music–Rosemarie Cook-Glover
Theater–Barbara Leonard
Staff Assistance–Victoria Bernal
Logo Design–Maureen Erbe

More About Aesthetics
Richard W. Burrows,
Executive Director,
Institute for Arts Education,
San Diego, California

Safe Use of Art Materials
Mary Ann Boykin, Visiting Lecturer,
Art Education; Director, The Art
School for Children and Young Adults,
University of Houston-Clear Lake,
Houston, Texas

Museum Education
Marilyn JS Goodman,
Director of Education,
Solomon R. Guggenheim Museum,
New York, New York

The National Museum of Women in the Arts Collection
National Museum of
Women in the Arts,
Washington, DC

Contributing Writer
Patricia Carter
Assistant Professor of Art Education
Georgia Southern University

Reviewers
Leslie Anderson
Teacher
Canopy Oaks Elementary School
Tallahassee, FL

Mary Ann Boykin
Visiting Lecturer, Art Education;
Director, The Art School for Children
and Young Adults
University of Houston-Clear Lake
Houston, TX

Cynthia M. Coleman
Kindergarten Teacher
Normandie Avenue School
Los Angeles Unified School District
Los Angeles, CA

Theresa Davis
Art Specialist
Fleming Island Elementary
Clay County School District
Orange Park, FL

Judy Gong
Multi-age Classroom Teacher
Pacific Elementary School
Lincoln Unified School District
Stockton, CA

Lori Groendyke Knutti
Art Educator
Harrison Street Elementary School
Big Walnut Elementary School
Sunbury, OH

Carol S. James
Kindergarten Teacher
Nitsch Elementary School
Klein Independent School District
Houston, TX

Laura McFadden
Art Supervisor
Briggs Elementary School
Florence District 1
Florence, SC

Steven R. Sinclair
Art Teacher
Big Country Elementary School
Southwest Independent School
District
San Antonio, TX

Connie Courtney Stephenson
Fine Arts Supervisor
Collier County School District
Naples, FL

Patti Wheeler
Teacher
N.B. Cook Elementary
School of the Arts
Escambia School District
Pensacola, FL

Student Activity Testers
Madeline Jobrack
Brady Woolridge
Emily Haupt
Matthew Ford
Abby McMillian
Christopher Byorth

TABLE OF CONTENTS

What Is Art? 8

Unit 1 Line

Introduction to Line 12

Lesson	Create Activity	Medium
1 Thick and Thin Lines	*Blanket Design*	Tempera 14
2 Different Kinds of Lines	*Circus Drawing*	Crayon 16
3 Looking at Smooth and Rough Lines	*Outdoors Painting*	Tempera 18
4 Lines to Touch	*Picture to Touch*	Textured Fibers 20
5 Broken Lines	*Animal Mosaic*	Cut Paper 22
6 Lines Make Pictures	*Self-Portrait*	Oil Pastel 24
Artsource Dance Lesson: Line in Dance		26
Wrapping Up Line		28

Unit 2 Shape

Introduction to Shape 30

Lesson	Create Activity	Medium
1 Lines Outline Shapes	*Space Creature*	Oil Pastel 32
2 Geometric Shapes	*Quilt Block*	Paper 34
3 Free-Form Shapes	*Free-Form Leaves*	Printing Ink 36
4 More About Shapes	*Inside-Outside Drawing*	Crayon 38
5 The Shape of Me	*Self-Portrait*	Markers 40
6 The Shape of My Family	*Family Picture*	Tempera Paint 42
Artsource Dance Lesson: Shape in Dance		44
Wrapping Up Shape		46

Unit 3 Color

Introduction to Color **48**

Lesson	Create Activity	Medium	
1 A Garden of Colors	*Flower Garden Drawing*	Crayon	**50**
2 Identifying Colors	*Sandwich Collage*	Paper	**52**
3 Looking at Colors	*Color Collage*	Magazine Pictures	**54**
4 Bright and Dull Colors	*Rain Forest Scene*	Oil Pastel/ Watercolor	**56**
5 Color and Feelings	*Creature of Your Own*	Watercolor/ Marker	**58**
6 Light and Dark Colors	*Sea Picture*	Tempera	**60**
Artsource Music Lesson: Color in Music			**62**
Wrapping Up Color			**64**

Unit 4 Space and Form

Introduction to Space and Form **66**

Lesson	Create Activity	Medium	
1 Space in Art	*Design Using Shapes*	Paper	**68**
2 Form	*Your Form*	Clay	**70**
3 A Building Is a Form	*Building*	Box/Paper	**72**
4 An Animal Is a Form	*Animal Form*	Clay	**74**
5 Forms Can Have Designs	*Make-Believe Creature*	Box/Marker	**76**
6 Forms Can Be Used	*Pinch Pot*	Clay	**78**
Artsource Theater Lesson: Form in Theater			**80**
Wrapping Up Space and Form			**82**

Unit 5 Texture

Introduction to Texture 84

Lesson	Create Activity	Medium
1 Texture You Can Touch	*Collage*	Textured Items 86
2 Texture You Can See	*Textured Hat*	Crayon 88
3 Designing with Texture	*Puppet*	Paper Bag/Fabric ... 90
4 Fiber Textures	*Basket Weaving*	Yarn 92
5 Real Texture in Forms	*Tile*	Clay 94
6 Texture in Shapes	*Stitchery Design*	Yarn 96

Artsource Theater Lesson: Texture in Theater 98

Wrapping Up Texture 100

Unit 6 Rhythm, Balance, and Unity

Introduction to Rhythm, Balance, and Unity 102

Lesson	Create Activity	Medium
1 Balance	*Drawing of a Face*	Marker 104
2 Even Balance with Animals	*Make-Believe Bug*	Tempera 106
3 Pattern and Rhythm	*Animals Drawing*	Crayon 108
4 Rhythm and Movement	*Train Painting*	Tempera 110
5 Rhythm and Printing	*Rain Forest Shape Print*	Tempera 112
6 Rhythm Helps Make Unity	*Neighborhood Mural*	Construction Paper/Marker 114

Artsource Music Lesson: Rhythm in Music 116

Wrapping Up Rhythm, Balance, and Unity 118

More About...

Technique Tips 120
Art Criticism 132
Aesthetics 136
Art History 140
Subject Matter 144
Seeing Lines, Shapes, and Size 148

Visual Index 154
Glossary 160
Index 166

FLORIDA WRITES! FL1

Expository Writing Practice FL2
Narrative Writing Practice FL5
Self Assessment FL8

What Is Art?

Art is...

Painting

Winslow Homer. (American). *Snap the Whip.* 1872. Oil on canvas. 12 × 20 inches. Metropolitan Museum of Art, New York, New York.

Drawing

Itō Jakuchū. (Japanese). *Fukurojin, the God of Longevity and Wisdom.* c. 1790. Hanging scroll, ink and light colors on paper. $43\frac{5}{8} \times 22\frac{1}{4}$ inches. Courtesty of Kimbell Art Museum, Fort Worth, Texas.

Sculpture

Artist unknown. (West Africa, Benin Kingdom). *Bronze head for the Altars of the Obas.* Mid-sixteenth century. Bronze. Superstock/Christies, London, England.

Architecture

Frank Lloyd Wright/Gwathmey, Siegel, and Associates. (American).*The Solomon R. Guggenheim Museum.* New York, New York.

Printmaking

Katsushika Hokusai. (Japanese). *The Great Wave Off Kanagawa.* 1831–33. Polychrome woodblock print. $10\frac{1}{8} \times 14\frac{15}{16}$ inches. Metropolitan Museum of Art, New York, New York.

Pottery

Artist unknown. Kiangsi Province (China). *Jar.* (Ming Dynasty). 1426–35. Porcelain painted in underglaze blue. 19 inches high. Metropolitan Museum of Art, New York, New York. Gift of Robert E. Todd, 1937.

Weaving

Artist unknown. (United States). *Appalachian Basket.* 1988. Split oak. 12 × 12 inches. Hudak private collection.

Toy Making

Artist unknown. (Russia). *Russian Doll.* 1991. Wood with oil paint. 8 inches high. Hudak private collection. Photograph by ©Tom Amedis.

Art is created by people.

Art talks with...

Line

Shape

Color

SPACE

FORM

TEXTURE

Rhythm

Balance

Unity

Unit 1

An Introduction to
Line

Katsushika Hokusai. (Japanese). *The Great Wave Off Kanagawa.* 1831–33. Polychrome woodblock print. $10\frac{1}{8} \times 14\frac{15}{16}$ inches. Metropolitan Museum of Art, New York, New York.

Artists use lines to create their artwork.

Can you find some different kinds of lines?

Artist Profile

Katsushika Hokusai
1760–1849

Self-Portrait.

Katsushika Hokusai

- was a Japanese artist.
- created prints.
- made landscapes.

Unit 1 Lesson 1

Thick and Thin Lines

Where do you see thick and thin lines in the picture?

Artist Unknown. Navajo (United States). *Classic Serape Style Wearing Blanket.* 1875. Plied cotton and Saxony wool. $73\frac{1}{2} \times 47$ inches. Utah Museum of Fine Arts, University of Utah, Salt Lake City, Utah.

Seeing like an artist

Find thick and thin lines on the walls and floor.

A **thick line** is wide.

A **thin line** is narrow.

Create

How would you use thick and thin lines to make a design?

Create a blanket for yourself with different lines.

Kristina Jimenez. Age 5. Tempera.

Lesson **1**

Unit 1 Lesson 2
Different Kinds of Lines

W. H. Brown. (American). *Bareback Riders*. 1886. Oil on cardboard mounted on wood. $18\frac{1}{2} \times 24\frac{1}{4}$ inches. National Gallery of Art, Washington, DC. Gift of Edgar William and Bernice Chrysler Garbisch. ©1996 Board of Trustees, National Gallery of Art, Washington, DC.

Find three different kinds of lines in the picture.

Seeing like an artist

Can you find straight, slanted, and curved lines around you?

Lines move in different directions.

straight   slanted   curved

Create

What lines do you see at a circus?

Draw a circus picture with different lines.

Ashley Weber. Age 5. *Monkey's Fun Time.* Marker and paint.

Lesson 2

Unit 1 Lesson 3

Looking at *Smooth* and Rough Lines

Tell what things in the art would feel smooth or rough.

Itō Jakuchū. (Japanese). *Fukurojin, the God of Longevity and Wisdom.* c. 1790. Hanging Scroll, ink and light colors on paper. $43\frac{5}{8} \times 22\frac{1}{4}$ inches. Courtesy of the Kimbell Art Museum, Fort Worth, Texas.

Seeing like an artist

Look around the room. Find something that looks smooth.

Lines that show how things feel to the touch look different.

smooth

rough

Create

What does your favorite outdoor place look like?

Paint it using smooth and rough lines.

Madeline Jobrack. Age 5. *Me, a Turtle, and a Swingset*. Tempera.

Lesson 3

Unit 1 Lesson 4

Lines to Touch

How would different parts in the picture feel if you could touch them?

Katsushika Hokusai. (Japanese). *Boy Juggling Shells*. Edo period. Album leaf, ink and color on paper. 13 5/16 × 9 1/2 inches. Metropolitan Museum of Art, New York, New York. Charles Stewart Smith Collection. Gift of Mrs. Charles Stewart Smith, in memory of Charles Stewart Smith, 1914.

Seeing like an artist

Trace lines in the air to show how your hair looks and feels.

Artists use **lines** to show how things feel.

Create

How can you make lines that feel different?

Create a picture with lines you can touch.

Francisco Calixto. Age 5. *Los Colores.* Glue, chalk, and pastel.

Lesson **4**

Unit 1 Lesson 5
Broken Lines

Artist Unknown. (Italy). *Ravenna Apse Mosaic (Detail)*. A.D. 549. The Church of Saint Apollinaris, Ravenna, Italy. Scala/Art Resource, New York.

Put your finger on a broken line in this art.

Seeing like an artist

Look at the wall and floor. Can you find broken lines?

Lines with spaces between them are **broken lines**.

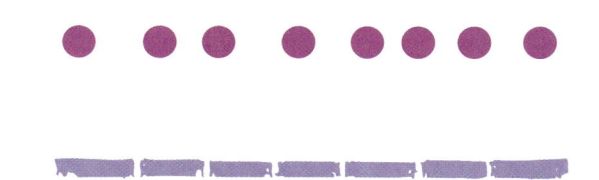

• •• • ••• •

Create

How would you make a picture with spaces between lines?

Draw some animals with broken lines.

Jessica M. Hopkins. Age 5. *Horse.* Construction paper.

Lesson 5

Unit 1 Lesson 6
Lines Make Pictures

Winslow Homer. (American). *Snap the Whip.* 1872. Oil on canvas. 12 × 20 inches. Metropolitan Museum of Art, New York, New York. Gift of Christian A. Zabriskie, 1950.

What things in the picture look like they are moving?

Seeing like an artist
Trace in the air one thing that you see. What kinds of lines did you make?

Some lines show things standing still.

Some lines show things moving.

Create

How would you show yourself moving in a picture?

Draw yourself playing.

Tiffany Palmer. Age 5. *Playing Soccer.* Crayon.

Lesson 6

Lines in Dance

Lewitzky Dance Company: Dancers in positions from "Impressions #2,"(Vincent van Gogh) a suite of dances choreographed by Bella Lewitzky, based on the painting *The Starry Night* by Vincent van Gogh. (Back L to R) Kimo Kimura, Kenneth Bowman; (Front) Kenneth B. Talley, John Pennington.

Bella Lewitzky creates dances. Her dancers make curved, straight, and slanted lines with their bodies.

What To Do

Make lines with your body.

1. Look at the painting. Name the kinds of lines you see.

2. Move your body to show each kind of line.

Vincent van Gogh. (Dutch). *The Starry Night.* 1889. Oil on canvas. $28\frac{3}{4} \times 36\frac{1}{2}$ inches. Museum of Modern Art. New York, New York.

Extra Credit

Use your body to make a moon or a star.

Dance

Wrapping Up Unit 1
Line

Reviewing Main Ideas

There are many kinds of lines.

You have seen and used different kinds of lines.

Hughie Lee-Smith. (American). *The Piper*. 1953. Oil on composition board. 55.9 × 89.5 cm. Photograph © The Detroit Institute of Arts, Detroit, Michigan. Gift of Mr. and Mrs. Stanley J. Winkleman. Licensed by VAGA, New York, New York.

Let's Visit a Museum

This museum is in Detroit. It has art from all over the world.

Summing Up

Look at the painting.

How many kinds of lines can you find?

The Detroit Institute of Art, Detroit, Michigan.

Unit 2

An Introduction to Shape

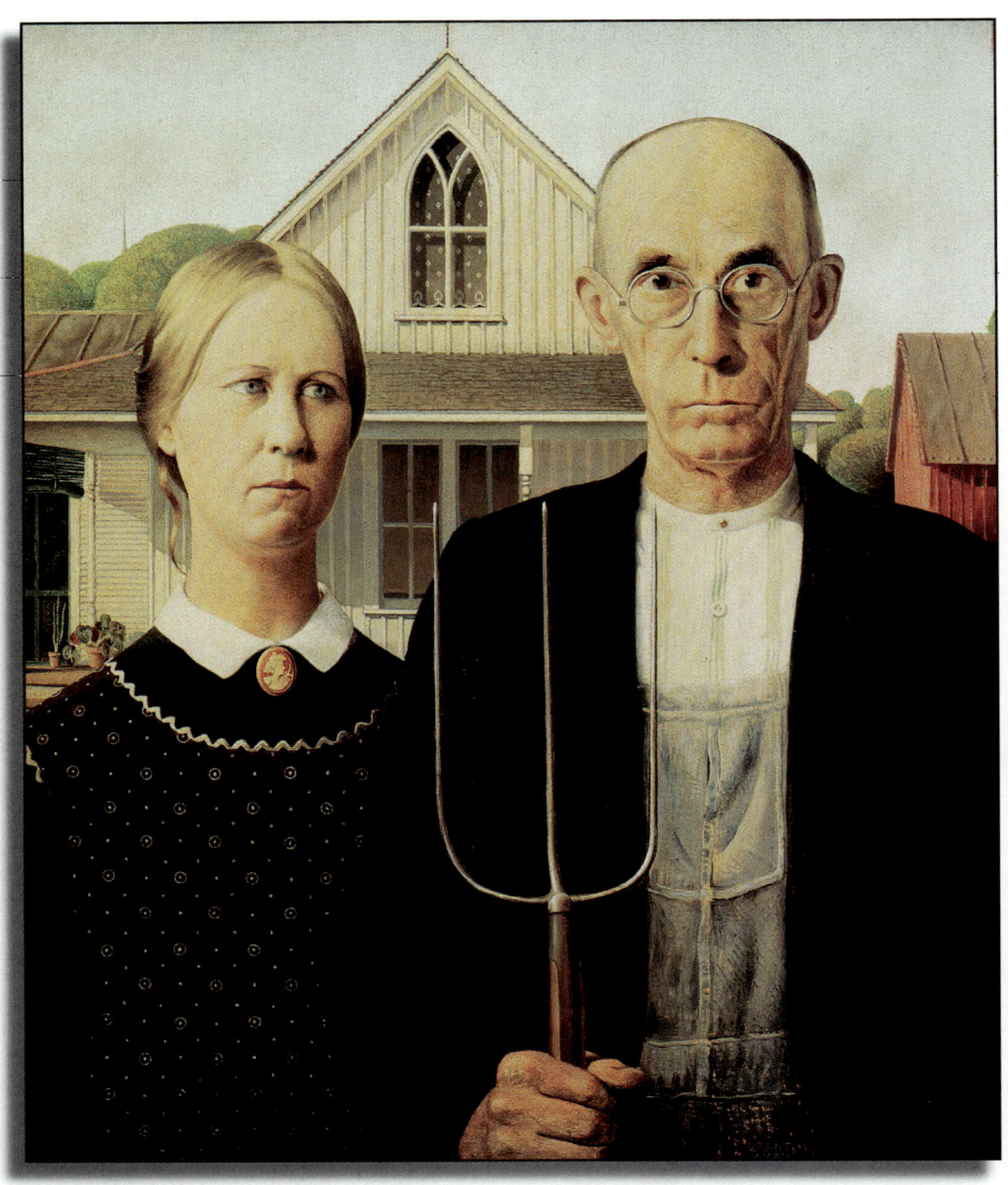

Grant Wood. (American). *American Gothic.* 1930. Oil on Beaverboard. 74.3 × 62.4 cm. The Art Institute of Chicago, Illinois. ©1998 Estate of Grant Wood/Licensed by VAGA, New York, New York.

A shape is made with a line that traces the edge of the shape.

What shapes can you find in the painting?

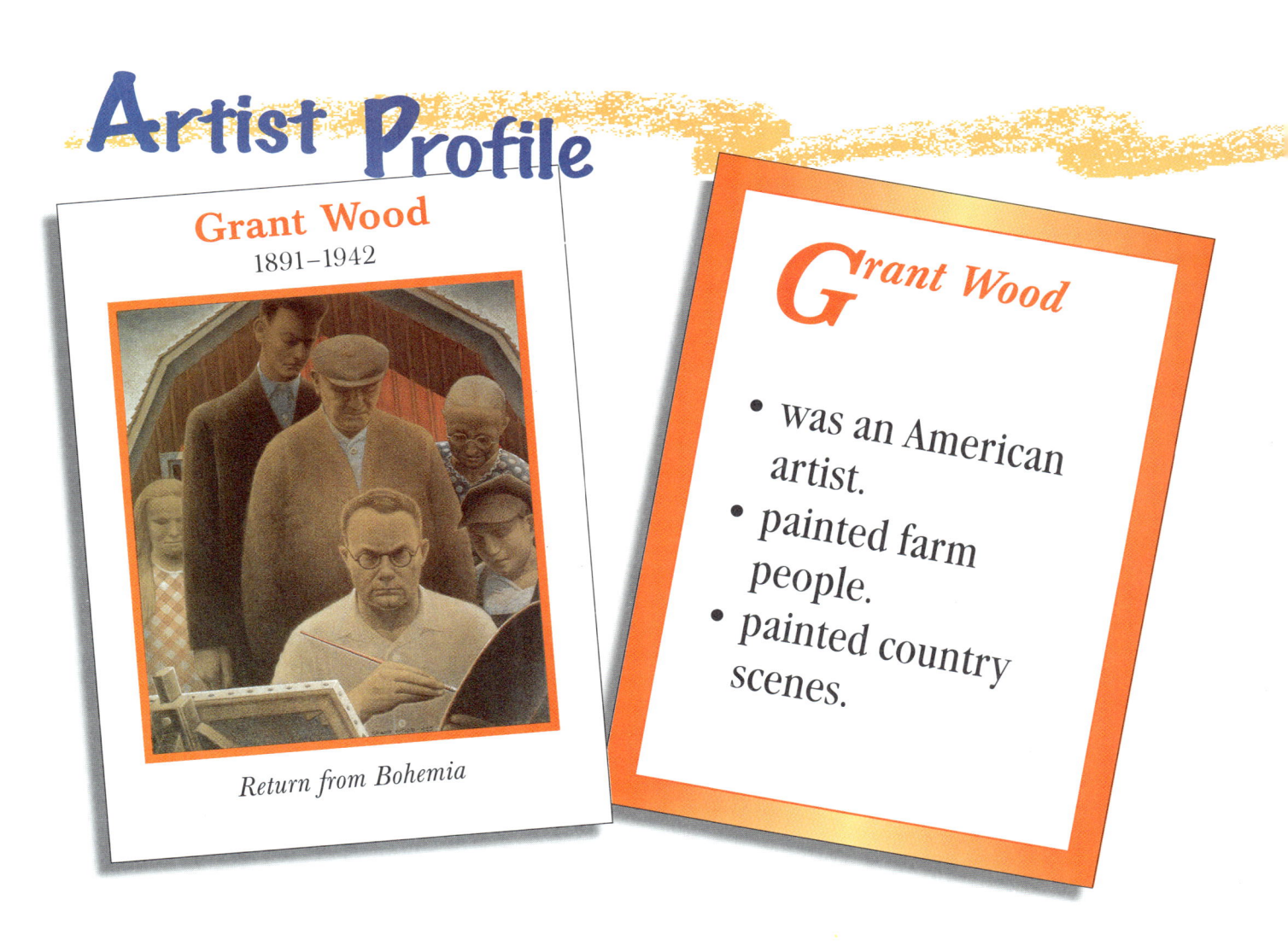

Artist Profile

Grant Wood
1891–1942

Return from Bohemia

Grant Wood

- was an American artist.
- painted farm people.
- painted country scenes.

Unit 2 Lesson 1
Lines Outline Shapes

Kenny Scharf. (American). *When Worlds Collide.* 1984. 10 feet, 2 inches × 17 feet, 5 inches. Courtesy of the Tony Shafrazi Gallery, New York, New York. © 1998 Kenny Scharf/Artists Rights Society (ARS), New York.

Trace with your finger the line around a shape you like in the painting.

Seeing like an artist
Trace a line around something near you. What shape did you make?

A line around the edge of a **shape** is the **outline**.

Create

What kinds of shapes do space creatures have?

Draw space creatures of your own.

Zoe Sommers. Age 6. *Space Creature*. Oil Pastel.

Lesson 1

Unit 2 Lesson 2
Geometric Shapes

Artist Unknown. (United States). *Album Quilt.* 1841–1844. Pieced and appliquéd cotton fabric. 82 × 75 inches. National Museum of American History, Smithsonian Institution, Washington, DC.

Point to all the geometric shapes on the quilt.

Seeing like an artist

Look at your clothes. Do you see a ■, a ▲, a ●, or a ▬?

34 Unit 2

Some shapes are **geometric shapes**.
Geometric shapes have names.

circle   square   triangle   rectangle

Create

What are your favorite geometric shapes?

Design a quilt with them.

Jeb Smith. Age 5. *The Slow Freight Train.* Construction paper and glue.

Lesson 2

Unit 2 Lesson 3

Free-Form Shapes

David Wiesner. (American). *Free Fall.* 1988. Illustration. Courtesy of Lothrop, Lee, and Shepard Books.

Point to the shapes in this painting that are not geometric shapes.

Seeing like an artist

Name a free-form shape you see. Trace the shape with your finger.

Artists use **free-form shapes** to show people, animals, and other things.

Create

Where do you see free-form shapes in nature?

Print some free-form leaves.

Steven Roth. Age 6. *Leaves of Nature*. Water-soluble printing ink.

Lesson **3**

37

Unit 2 Lesson 4
More About Shapes

Allan Rohan Crite. (American). *School's Out*. 1936. Oil on canvas. $30\frac{1}{4} \times 36\frac{1}{8}$ inches. National Museum of American Art, Smithsonian Institution, Washington, DC.

Find different shapes in this painting and name them.

Seeing like an artist

Name one thing you use in school. Is the shape geometric or free-form?

It's easy to find **geometric shapes** and **free-form shapes**. They're everywhere.

Create

How many geometric shapes and free-form shapes can you find?

Draw an inside-outside picture.

Madison Hendrix. Age 6. *Picture Frame.* Crayon.

Lesson **4**

Unit 2 Lesson 5

THE SHAPE OF ME

William H. Johnson. (American). *Li'l Sis*. 1944. Oil on paperboard. 26 × 21¼ inches. National Museum of American Art, Smithsonian Institution, Washington, DC. Art Resource, NY.

Artists use different shapes to show body parts. Name the body parts of the girl.

Seeing like an artist

Is your hand a free-form or a geometric shape?

Body parts are different shapes.
All body parts are **free-form shapes**.

Create

How many free-form shapes does your body have?

Draw a big picture of yourself.

Stephanie Gowdy. Age 6. *Myself*. Tempera and chalk.

Lesson 5

41

Unit 2 Lesson 6

THE SHAPE OF MY FAMILY

Ralph Earl. (American). *Mrs. Noah Smith and Her Family.* c. 1780. Oil on canvas. 64 × 85¾ inches. Metropolitan Museum of Art, New York, New York. Gift of Edgar William and Bernice Chrysler Garbisch, 1964.

Point to the smallest person in the painting. Point to the biggest.

Seeing like an artist

Who is the tallest person in your room?

42   Unit 2

People are all different sizes. The **shapes** used to draw people are different sizes.

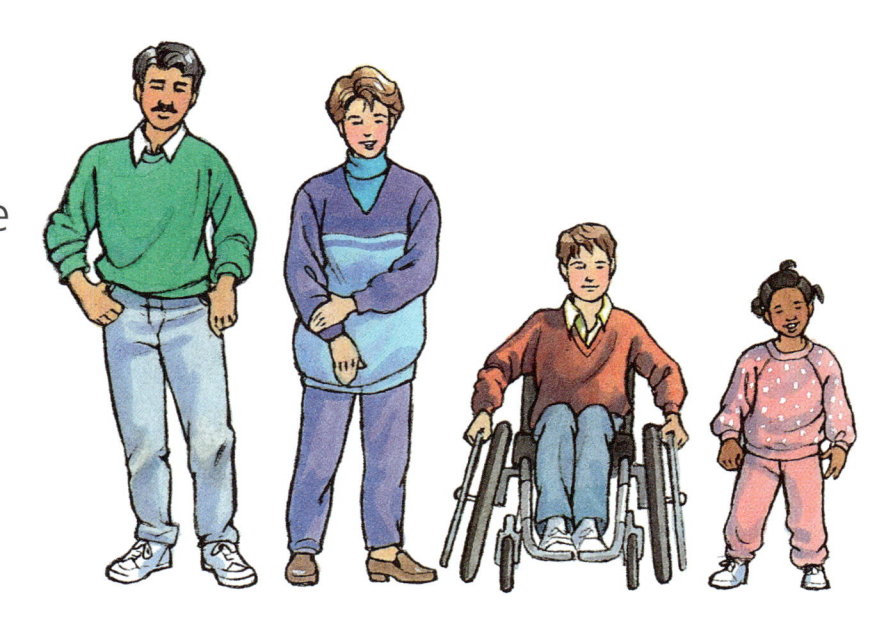

Create

How many different people sizes do you have in your family?

Draw a picture of them.

Allie Berlin. Age 5. *My Family*. Crayon.

Lesson **6**

Shape in Dance

AMAN International Folk Ensemble: "Suite of Appalachian Music and Dance."

Jerry Duke creates dances. His dancers make lots of circles. His dancers sometimes work with puppets.

What To Do

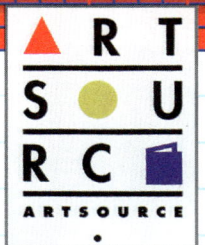

Create circle shapes and forms.

1. Draw five circles of different sizes.

2. Make circles with your body.

3. Make circles with a partner.

4. Make circles with a group.

Extra Credit

Practice the circles you made with your body.
Perform them for a group.

Dance

Wrapping Up Unit 2
Shape

Reviewing Main Ideas

Lines outline shapes.

There are geometric shapes and free-form shapes.

Pieter Bruegel the Elder. (Dutch). *Children's Games.* 1560. Oil on oakwood panel. $46\frac{1}{2} \times 63\frac{3}{8}$ inches. Kunsthistarisches Museum, Gemaeldegalerie, Vienna, Austria. Photograph by Erich Lessing, Art Resource, NY.

Summing Up

F*ind* the shapes in the painting.

Can you name them?

Careers in Art

Jerry Pinkney began drawing when he was four years old. Now he makes beautiful pictures for books.

Jerry Pinkney, book illustrator.

47

Unit 3

An Introduction to *Color*

Henri Matisse. (French). *Purple Robe and Anemones.* 1937. Oil on canvas. 73.1 × 60.3 cm. The Baltimore Museum of Art: The Cone Collection, formed by Dr. Claribel Cone and Miss Etta Cone of Baltimore, Maryland. ©1998 Succession H. Matisse, Paris/Artists Rights Society (ARS), New York.

Colors are everywhere.

What colors in the painting can you name?

Artist Profile

Henri Matisse
1869–1954

Henri Matisse

- was a great French artist.
- loved to paint bright colors.

Unit 3 Lesson 1

A Garden of Colors

Peggy Flora Zalucha. (American). *Sprinkler Garden* (diptych part 1). 1994. Transparent watercolor on paper. 36 × 52 inches. Courtesy of Peggy Flora Zalucha.

Name the colors of the flowers in this garden scene.

Seeing like an artist

Look around you. What colors do you see?

Colors have names.

Red   Orange    Yellow    Green    Blue

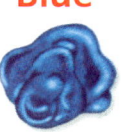

Purple    Brown    Black    White

Create

What colors would you put in your garden?

Draw your own flower garden.

Lauren Knutti. Age 5. Pencil and crayon.

Lesson 1

51

Unit 3 Lesson 2
Identifying Colors

Claes Oldenburg. (Swedish). *Two Cheeseburgers With Everything (Dual Hamburgers)*. 1962. Burlap soaked in plaster, painted with enamel. $7 \times 14\frac{3}{4} \times 8\frac{5}{8}$ inches. The Museum of Modern Art, New York, New York. The Philip Johnson Fund. Photograph © 1998 The Museum of Modern Art, New York.

What kind of foods do you see in this artwork?

Seeing like an artist

Look around you. What objects do you see that are the color red?

Colors help us identify things.

Create

What do you like on your sandwiches?

Design a colorful sandwich **collage**.

Riane Ramsey. Age 5. *My Yummy Lunch*. Paper Collage.

Lesson 2

53

Unit 3 Lesson 3

Looking at Colors

Wayne Thiebaud. (American). *Jawbreaker Machine.* 1963. Oil on canvas. 26 × 31½ inches. Nelson-Atkins Museum of Art, Kansas City, Missouri. Gift of Mr. and Mrs. Jack Glenn through the Friends of Art.

Name the colors the artist used in the **painting**.

Seeing like an artist

What colors would you use to paint your favorite toy?

Artists use colors from real life to make artwork look real.

Create

Where do you see your favorite colors?

Create a color collage.

Susan Morris. Age 5. *Blue.* Cut paper.

Lesson 3

55

Unit 3 Lesson 4
Bright and Dull Colors

Lynne Cherry. (American). *The Great Kapok Tree.* 1990. Illustration. © Lynne Cherry.

Where do you see bright colors and dull colors in the painting?

Seeing like an artist

Stand next to a classmate. Is your shirt color brighter or darker?

Shapes stand out when you use **bright colors**. **Dull colors** make shapes hide.

Create

Name some places where you see many different colors.

Draw a rain forest scene.

Chloe Paddison. Age 5. *Rain Forest.* Oil pastel and watercolor.

Lesson 4

57

Unit 3 Lesson 5

Color and Feelings

Artist unknown. (China). *Jar.* (Ming Dynasty). 1426-35. Porcelain painted in underglaze blue. 19 inches high. Metropolitan Museum of Art, New York, New York.

How do you feel when you look at the dragon on this vase?

Seeing like an artist

Name a creature you have seen in a cartoon. What color is it?

Artists use **bright colors** to make us feel happy. **Dull colors** can make us feel sad or scared.

Create

How do different colors make you feel?

Paint a creature with colors you like.

Camron Nobles. Age 5. *Land of the Lost*. Watercolor and marker.

Lesson 5

Unit 3 Lesson 6
Light and Dark Colors

Graeme Base. (English). *Act II, Scene 1 "The Deep."* (From the book *The Sign of the Sea Horse*). 1992. Illustration. Courtesy of Harry N. Abrams.

Point to a dark blue part of the painting. Now point to a light blue part.

Seeing like an artist

Look in a book. Find a picture that has light blue and dark blue.

Mixing colors with black or white makes them **darker** or **lighter**.

Create

What things in the sea have light and dark colors?

Create a sea picture with light and dark colors.

Jeanette Gutierrez. Age 6. *Fish*. Tempera.

Lesson 6

Color in Music

Paul Salamunovich, Artistic Director for the Los Angeles Master Chorale.

Paul Salamunovich is a choral conductor. He leads people in singing songs. He tells people when to sing fast or slow, soft or loud.

62 Unit 3

What To Do

Take a song you know and change the way you sing it.

1. Choose one song you know.
2. Sing the song in different ways.
3. Choose the color that best fits your song.

Extra Credit

Sing a new song. Tell why the color best fits your song.

Wrapping Up Unit 3

Color

Reviewing Main Ideas

Colors have names.

Colors help us identify things.

Marc Chagall. (Russian). *Paris Through the Window*. 1913. Oil on canvas. $53\frac{1}{2} \times 55\frac{1}{4}$ inches. Solomon R. Guggenheim Museum. New York, New York.

Let's Visit a Museum

This museum is in New York City. Part of the building is round.

Summing Up

T*he* artist used many colors to create this painting. Name the colors.

Solomon R. Guggenheim Museum. New York, New York.

Unit 4

An Introduction to Space and Form

Alexander Calder. (American). *Calder's Circus.* 1926–31. Mixed Media. 54 × 94$\frac{1}{4}$ × 95$\frac{1}{4}$ inches. Collection of Whitney Museum of American Art, New York, New York. Purchase, with funds from a public fundraising campaign in May, 1982. /©1998 Artists Rights Society (ARS), New York/ADAGP, Paris.

A form is a solid shape that takes up space.

What forms do you see in this artwork?

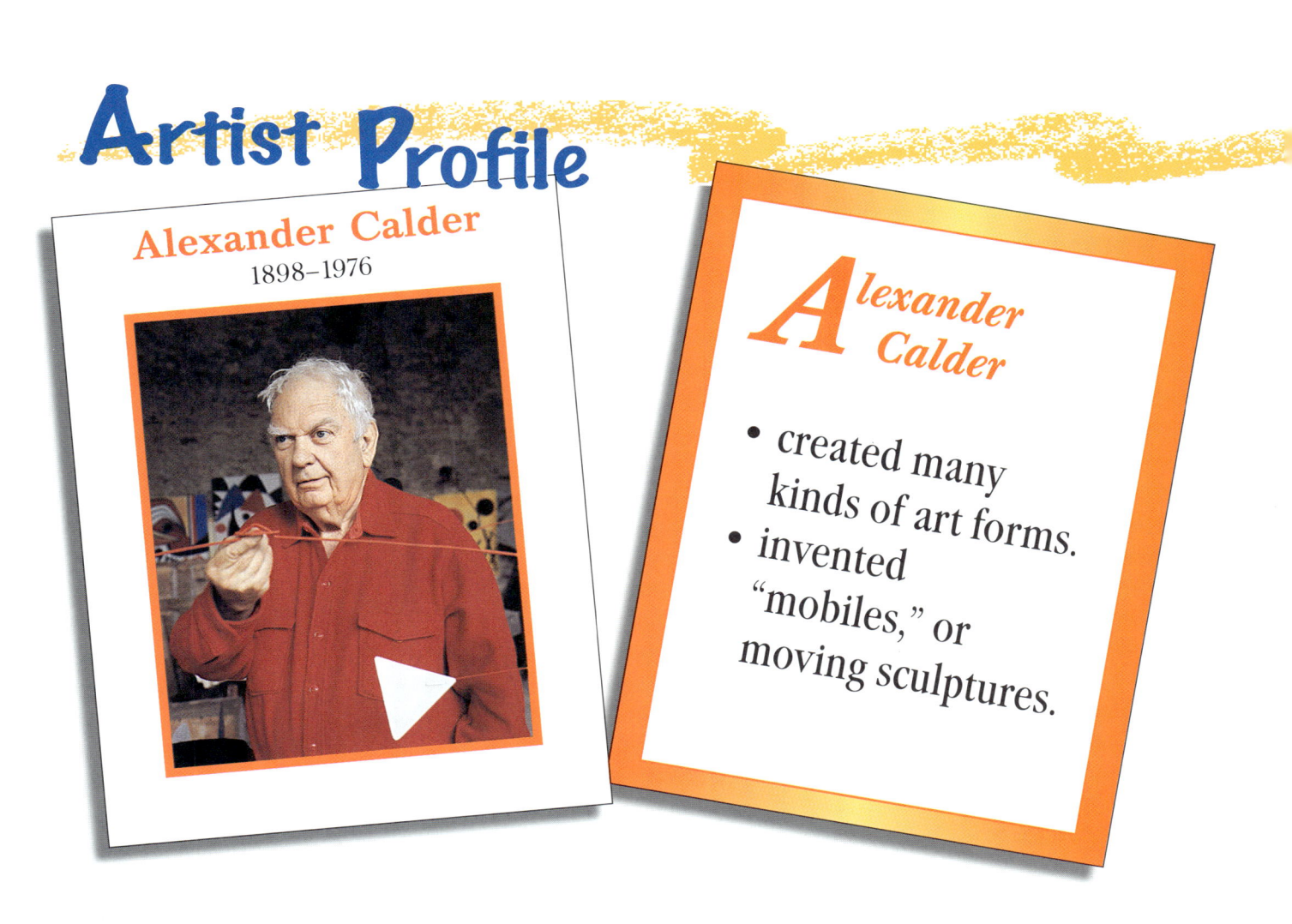

Artist Profile

Alexander Calder
1898–1976

Alexander Calder

- created many kinds of art forms.
- invented "mobiles," or moving sculptures.

Unit 4 Lesson 1
Space in Art

Dorothea Rockburne. (Canadian). *Sheba*. 1980. Gesso, oil, conte crayon, and glue on linen. 74 × 59½ inches. The National Museum of Women in the Arts, Washington, DC. Gift of Wallace and Wilhelmina Holladay. © 1998 Dorothea Rockburne. Artists Rights Society (ARS), New York.

Point to the empty areas around the shapes in this artwork.

Seeing like an artist

Do you see space around the clouds when you look in the sky?

The empty places around and between shapes are called **space**.

Create

How could you show space on paper?

Create a design using shapes.

Alberto Barojas. Age 5. *Shapes.* Crayons and cut paper.

Lesson **1**

Unit 4 Lesson 2
Form

Felipa Trujillo. (American). *Man.* Early 1900s. From the Girard Foundation Collection, in the Museum of International Folk Art, a unit of the Museum of New Mexico, Santa Fe, New Mexico. Photographer: Michel Monteaux.

This form is a **sculpture**. Describe what you think it would look like from all sides.

Seeing like an artist

What are the different sides of a form you see in your classroom?

A form is solid.
You can look all around a form.

Create

What do you look like from different sides?

Create a form of you.

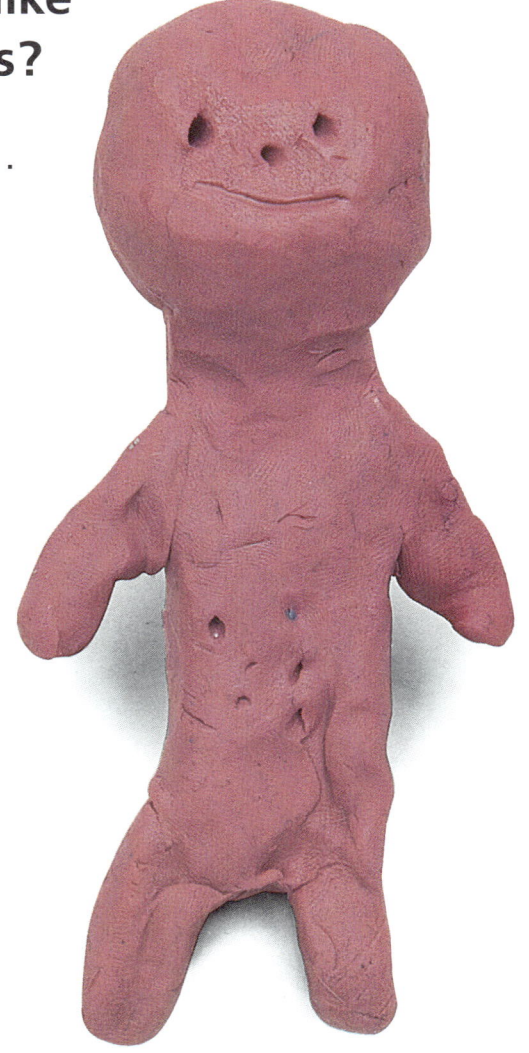

Brady Wooldridge. Age 5. *Happy Me.* Clay.

Lesson 2

Unit 4 Lesson 3

A Building Is a Form

Name some of the different parts of this building.

Artist unknown. (Poland). *Szopka*. c. 1960. Foil over cardboard. $50\frac{1}{4}$ inches high. Museum of International Folk Art, Santa Fe, New Mexico.

Seeing like an artist

What parts of your school building do you see from outside?

A building is a **form**. You can walk around a building and see all the parts.

Create

What kinds of buildings have you seen?

Design your own building.

Isaac Justus. Age 5. *A Little House.* Milk carton, markers, and cut paper.

Lesson **3**

Unit 4 Lesson 4

An Animal Is a Form

Artist unknown. (Egypt). *Ancient Egyptian Hippo "William."* 1991–1786 B.C. Faience. 11 × 20 cm. Metropolitan Museum of Art, New York, New York. Gift of Edward S. Harkness, 1917.

What kind of animal form do you see in the picture?

Seeing like an artist

What other animals with four legs could be made as a sculpture?

An animal **sculpture** is a **form**. You can walk around this animal form and see all four legs.

Create

What do your favorite animals look like?

Design an animal form.

Caitlin Cornwell. Age 5. *Slowie.* Clay and tempera.

Lesson 4

75

Unit 4 Lesson 5

Forms Can Have Designs

Name the things the artist used when designing this giraffe.

Artist unknown. (American). *Bottle Cap Giraffe.* 1966. Carved and painted wood, bottle caps, rubber, glass, animal hair, and fur. $72\frac{1}{2} \times 54 \times 17$ inches. National Museum of American Art, Smithsonian Institution, Washington, DC.

Seeing like an artist

Where else have you seen animals with designs?

Artists can turn different **forms** into make-believe creatures.

Create

What materials would you use to design your creature?

Create a make-believe creature.

Sarah Martin. Age 6. *My Critter.* Mixed media.

Lesson **5**

Unit 4 Lesson 6
Forms Can Be Used

How would you use the jar in this picture?

Artist unknown. (China). *Painted Storage Jar.* c. 2500–1700 B.C. Clay, iron oxide, and magnesium pigments. 15 inches high × 16 inches in diameter. Kimbell Art Museum, Fort Worth, Texas.

Seeing like an artist

Where do you see forms that are pretty and useful?

Jars and bowls are an **art form** that people look at and use.

Create

How could you design an artwork to use at home?

Create a pinch pot.

Elizabeth Sterling Morris. Age 5. *My Holding Bowl.* Clay.

Lesson **6**

Form in Theater

Sandy Spieler is the leader of a puppet and mask theater. She and other people are in a May Day parade. They bring giant puppets that they made.

In the Heart of the Beast Puppet and Mask Theatre: Dragon puppet in May Day Parade and Festival.

What To Do

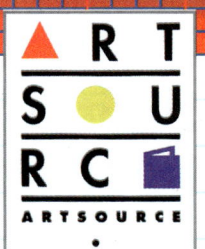

Use your body to move like an animal.

1. Choose an animal. Think about how the animal moves.

2. Show how the animal moves. Practice being the animal.

3. Share your animal moves with the class.

Extra Credit

Make the sound a real animal makes. Ask others to move like that animal.

Theater

Wrapping Up Unit 4
Space and Form

Reviewing Main Ideas

A form is a solid shape that takes up space.

You can see a form from all sides.

Artist unknown. (Russian). *Russian Nesting Doll.* 1991. Wood with oil paint. 8 inches high. Hudak private collection.

Careers in Art

When Chris Down was a little boy, he liked to draw and build things. Now he designs new toys.

Summing Up

T*he* space inside the form of the doll is filled with smaller dolls.

What kind of form is the doll?

Chris Down, toy designer.

Unit 5
An Introduction to
Texture

Harriet Powers. (American). *Bible Quilt, Detail: Dark Day of May 19, 1817.* Pieced and appliquéd cotton embroidered with plain and metallic yarns. 69 × 105 inches (overall). Courtesy of the Museum of Fine Arts, Boston, Massachusetts.

Texture is the way something feels.

How do you think this quilt, or blanket, feels to the touch?

Artist Profile

Harriet Powers
1837–1911

Harriet Powers
- was African American.
- made many quilts that told family stories.

Unit 5 Lesson 1
Texture You Can Touch

Betty Parsons. (American). *Winged Frog.* 1978. Mixed-media wood construction. 27 × 20 inches. The National Museum of Women in the Arts, Washington, DC. Gift of Wallace and Wilhelmina Holladay.

This frog is made of wood. Point to the part of the frog that you think feels rough.

Seeing like an artist
Describe how textures in your classroom feel.

Something you can feel with your fingers is called **real texture**.

Create

How many different textures can you put in a collage?

Create a collage with textures.

Dillon Jones. Age 6. *House and Yard.* Mixed media.

Lesson 1

Unit 5 Lesson 2
Texture You Can See

How do you think the child's hat would feel to touch?

Gabriele Münter. (German). *Child with Ball.* c. 1916. Oil on canvas. 20½ × 17 inches. The National Museum of Women in the Arts, Washington, DC. On loan from the Wallace and Wilhelmina Holladay Collection/© 1988. © 1996 Artists Rights Society (ARS), New York/VG Bild-Kunst, Bonn.

Seeing like an artist

How could you draw the texture of something you see?

88 Unit 5

Texture you can see but cannot touch is **visual texture**.

Create

How can you show how different things feel?

Design a hat that has different textures.

David Belk. Age 5. *Top Hat*. Crayon.

Lesson 2

89

Unit 5 Lesson 3
Designing with Texture

Artist unknown. (Western Europe). *Hand Puppets.* Late nineteenth century. Painted wood. 16 inches high (on average). Museum of International Folk Art, Santa Fe, New Mexico.

Name the kinds of textures you see on the heads and bodies of these puppets.

Seeing like an artist

Tell about the textures of a puppet you have seen.

Cloth and yarn have different **textures**.

smooth   rough   bumpy

fuzzy   scratchy

Create

Where would you place different textures on a puppet?

Create a puppet with textures.

Jay Warden. Age 5. *Nojay*. Paper bag, buttons, and material.

Lesson 3

Unit 5 Lesson 4
Fiber Textures

Artist unknown. (United States). *Appalachian Basket.* 1988. 12 × 12 inches. Split Oak. Hudak Private Collection.

How do you think the basket shown here feels to the touch?

Seeing like an artist

Straw is a fiber. What other fibers could be used to weave a basket?

92   Unit 5

Wood, straw, and grass are **fibers**
Many fibers are found in nature.

Create

What fibers would you use to make a basket of your own?

Weave a basket.

Olivia Carter. Age 5. *Baskets to Hold Things.* Plastic cups and yarn.

Lesson 4

Unit 5 Lesson 5

Real Texture in Forms

Artist unknown. Ashanti people (Ghana). *Fish, Gold Weight*. Nineteenth–twentieth century. Brass. $3\frac{1}{2}$ inches high. Metropolitan Museum of Art, New York, New York.

What do you think this fish would feel like if you could touch it?

Seeing like an artist

What kinds of lines would you use to make a clay tiger?

Tools or objects can be used to add **texture** to artwork. The texture that you can feel is called **real texture**.

Create

What objects would you use to show real texture?

Create a tile with real texture.

Thomas Harding. Age 5. *My Birthday Cake.* Clay, string, and beads.

Lesson 5

95

Unit 5 Lesson 6
Texture in Shapes

Patty Coggeshall. (American). *Sampler.* c. 1792. Linen embroidered with silk thread. $19\frac{1}{2} \times 16\frac{5}{8}$ inches. The Metropolitan Museum of Art, Rogers Fund, 1913.

Point to the shapes this artist created with yarn on the cloth. This art is called **stitchery**.

Seeing like an artist

What shapes did the artist stitch in the picture?

Artists sew yarn to add **real texture** to artwork.

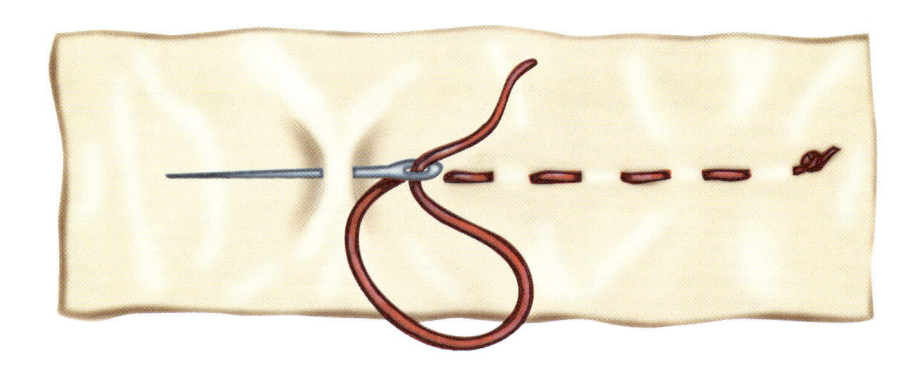

Create

What kinds of designs can you sew on cloth?

Sew your own design.

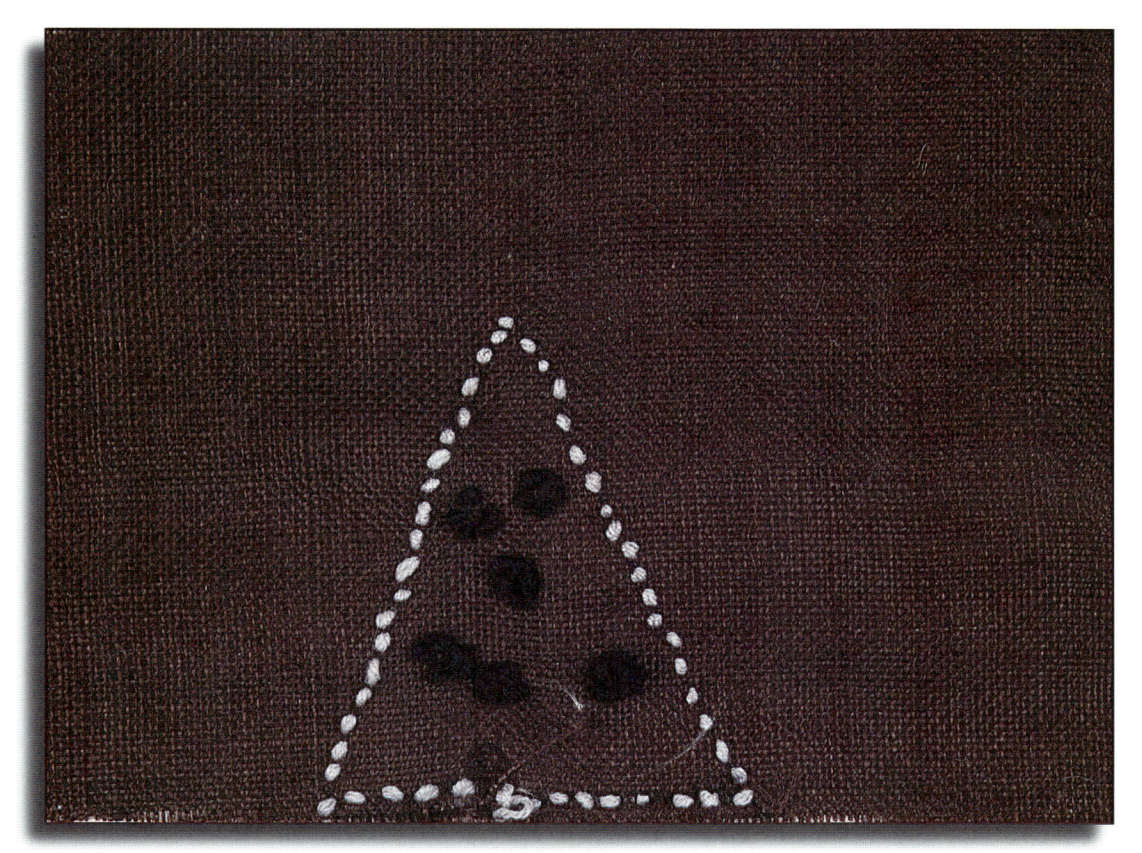

Kara Bloom. Age 5. *Pyramid.* Burlap and yarn.

Lesson 6

97

Texture in Theater

Geri Keams, storyteller.

Geri Keams is a storyteller. One story she tells is about a girl who sews porcupine quills on buckskin. The name of the story is "The Quillwork Girl."

What To Do

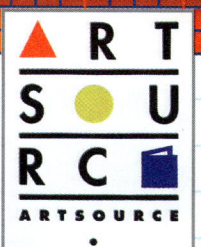

Tell a story.

1. Listen to a story.
2. Talk about the story.
3. Role-play the story with others.

Extra Credit

Draw your favorite part of the story.

Theater

Wrapping Up Unit 5

Texture

Reviewing Main Ideas

You feel real texture with your hand.

You see visual texture with your eyes.

Artist unknown. (West Africa, Benin Kingdom). *Bronze Head for the Altars of the Obas.* Mid-sixteenth century. Bronze. Nelson-Atkins Museum, Kansas City, Missouri. ©Superstock/Christies, London, England.

Let's Visit a Museum

This museum is in Kansas City. It has art from all over the world.

Summing Up

This sculpture has real texture. How do you think it would feel?

Nelson-Atkins Museum, Kansas City, Missouri.

Unit 6

An Introduction to

Rhythm, Balance, and Unity

Maria Martínez. (American). *Two Black-on-Black Pots.* Ceramic. Courtesy of Maria Martínez, ©Jerry Jacka Photography.

An artist can repeat lines, shapes, or patterns in an artwork.

What has the artist repeated on the pottery?

Artist Profile

Maria Martínez
1887–1980

Maria Martínez

- was from New Mexico.
- was a Pueblo potter.
- Her husband decorated her pottery.

Unit 6 Lesson 1
Balance

Chuck Close. (American). *Self Portrait.* 1987. Oil on canvas. 72 × 60 inches. Photograph courtesy of Pace Wildenstein Gallery, New York, New York. Photo by Bill Jacobson.

How can you tell that the face of this man has even balance?

Seeing like an artist

Study the face of your teacher. Tell why it is balanced.

Fold a shape in half. When both halves are exactly the same, the shape has **even balance**.

Create

How does your face look in the mirror?

Draw it to show even balance.

Cecilia Lennox. Age 5. *Buttons*. Marker and buttons.

Lesson 1

105

Unit 6 Lesson 2
Even Balance with Animals

Artist unknown. (China). *Butterfly*. c. 1950. Cut paper. $8\frac{1}{2} \times 15\frac{1}{8}$ inches. Museum of International Folk Art, Santa Fe, New Mexico. From the Girard Foundation Collection in the Museum of International Folk Art, a unit of the Museum of New Mexico. Photographer: Michel Monteaux.

One half of this butterfly looks the same as the other half. Point to the parts on each half.

Seeing like an artist

How many other animals can you name that have even balance?

An animal has **even balance**. The left half and the right half of an animal are the same.

Create

What would a bug with even balance look like?

Create a make-believe bug.

Karel Davis. Age 6. *Bug.* Tempera.

Lesson **2**

107

Unit 6 Lesson 3

Pattern and Rhythm

Artist unknown. Kuna (Panama). *Mola.* Twentieth century. Layered and cut fabric with stitchery. Hudak private collection. Photograph by ©Frank Fortune.

This artist uses shapes, lines, and colors. Find them.

Seeing like an artist

Find lines, shapes, and colors that repeat in your clothes.

Repeating a line, a **shape**, or a color in artwork creates a **visual rhythm**.

Create

How can you create a visual rhythm in an artwork?

Draw a parade of animals.

Caycee Creamer. Age 5. *Animal Parade*. Marker.

Lesson 3

Unit 6 Lesson 4

Rhythm and Movement

Jack Savitsky. (American). *Train in Coal Town.* 1968. Oil on fiberboard. 31¼ × 47¾ inches. National Museum of American Art, Smithsonian Institution, Washington, DC. Art Resource, New York.

What shapes did the artist repeat in this painting?

Seeing like an artist

What shapes would you repeat to show a car or a boat moving?

110 Unit 6

Repeated shapes will create a sense of **rhythm** and **movement**.

Create

How can you draw something to show movement?

Paint a moving train.

Travis Adkins. Age 5. *Train.* Oil pastel.

Lesson 4

111

Unit 6 Lesson 5

Rhythm and Printing

Artist unknown. (Kenya). *Printed Fabric from Bambalulu Handcraft Center.* 1993. Cotton with gold fabric ink. 2 × 2½ feet. Private Collection.

Find the animal that is repeated on this cloth. How do you think the artist repeated this shape?

Seeing like an artist

Think of an animal. What shapes would you use to draw it?

Pressing a shape from one thing to another many times is called **printing**.

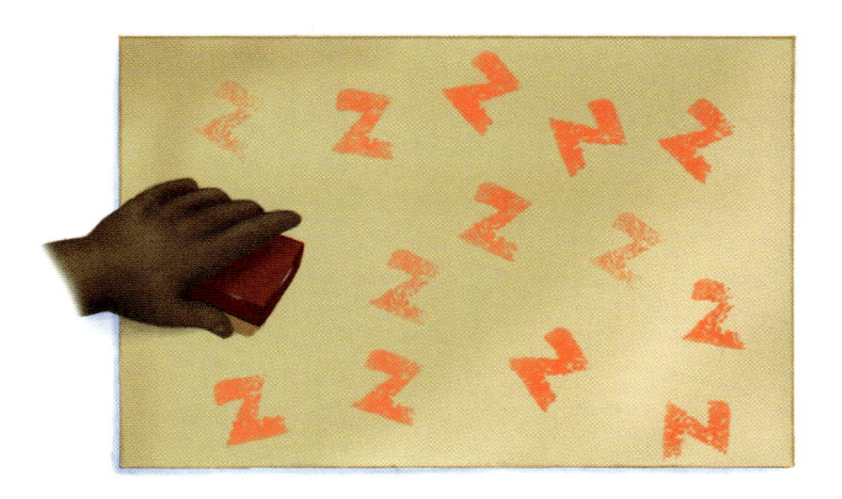

Create

What kinds of shapes would you find in a rain forest?

Print a rain forest shape.

Josh Phillips. Age 6. *Blue Leaves.* Stamp and tempera.

Lesson 5

Unit 6 Lesson 6
Rhythm Helps Make Unity

What shapes are repeated in this artwork? Name them.

John Biggers. (American). *Shotguns, Fourth Ward.* 1987. Acrylic and oil on board. 41¾ × 32 inches. Hampton University Museum, Hampton, Virginia.

Seeing like an artist

What shapes do you see repeated in your school?

Repeated shapes and colors create a feeling of **unity**, or belonging together.

Create

What kinds of shapes are repeated in your neighborhood?

Create a **mural** about your neighborhood.

Williamston Primary School. Ages 5–6. *All Through the Town.* Tempera.

Lesson 6

115

Rhythm in Music

Chic Street Man, musician.

Chic Street Man sings and plays the guitar. He writes his own songs. His songs tell stories.

Unit 6

What To Do

Show the rhythm of a nursery rhyme.

1. Say a nursery rhyme.
2. Clap your hands to the nursery rhyme.
3. Stamp your feet to the nursery rhyme.

Extra Credit

Do a pantomime of the nursery rhyme.

Music

Wrapping Up Unit 6
Rhythm, Balance, and Unity

Reviewing Main Ideas

A shape has even balance when both halves are the same.

Repeating a line, a shape, or a color in art creates visual rhythm.

Repeated shapes and colors create a feeling of unity, or belonging together.

Berthe Morisot. (French). *The Sisters*. 1869. Oil on canvas. $20\frac{1}{2} \times 32$ inches. Gift of Mrs. Charles S. Carstairs, ©1996 Board of Trustees, National Gallery of Art, Washington, DC.

Careers in Art

Berthe Morisot lived a long time ago. She earned her living as an artist.

Summing Up

M*orisot* repeated lines, shapes, and colors to create rhythm in the painting.

What is the same on both sides of this picture?

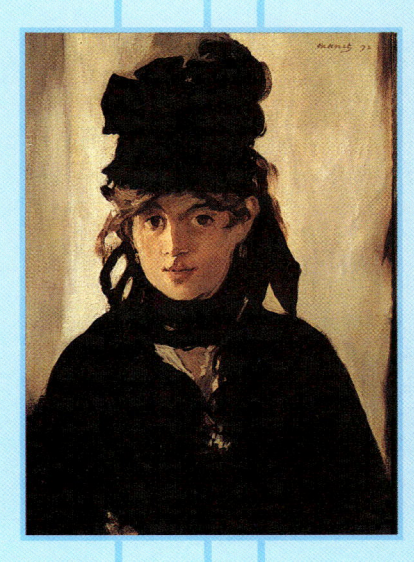

Berthe Morisot, painter

More About...
Technique Tips

Drawing

Pencil

Thin lines.

Thick lines.

Crayon

Thin lines.

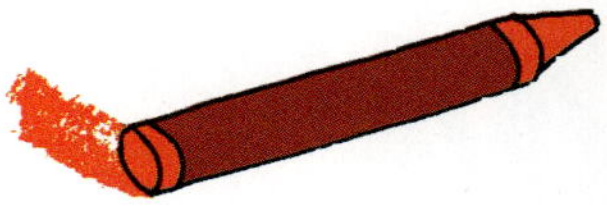

Thick lines.

Small dots.

Large dots.

Large spaces.

Marker

Use the tip.

Use the side of the tip.

Put on the cap.

More About...Technique Tips

More About... Technique Tips

Oil Pastels

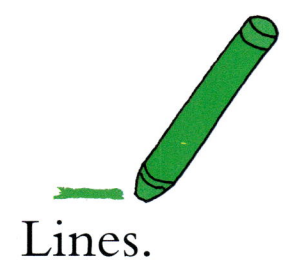

Lines.

Color in large spaces.

Blend colors.

Colored Chalk

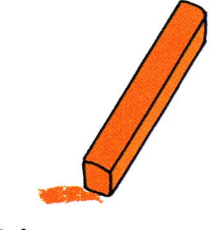

Lines.

Color in large spaces.

Blend colors.

More About...Technique Tips

More About... Technique Tips

Painting

Taking Care of Your Paintbrush

Rinse and blot to change colors.
Clean your brush when you are done.

1. Rinse.

2. Wash with soap.

3. Rinse again and blot.

4. Shape.

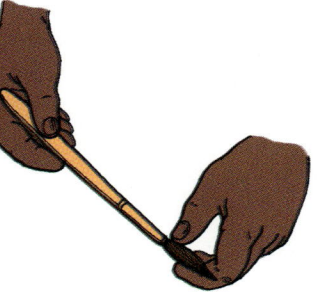

5. Store.

More About...
Technique Tips

Tempera

Wipe your brush.

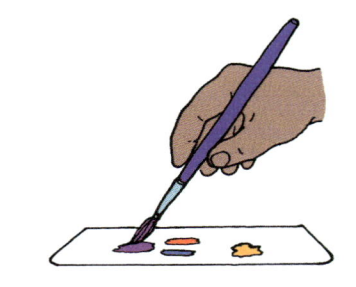

Mix on a palette.

Use a wide brush for large spaces.

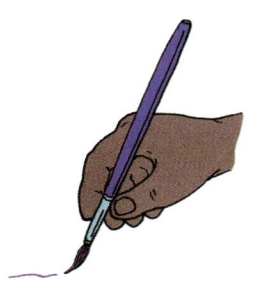

Use a thin, pointed brush for details.

More About...Technique Tips 123

More About... Technique Tips

Watercolor

Put water on each color.

Dip the brush in the paint.

Mix on a separate palette.

Press firmly for thick lines.

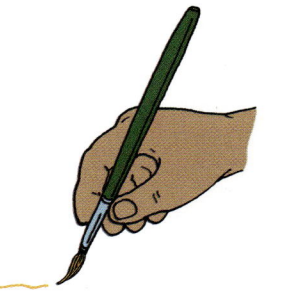

Press lightly for thin lines.

Watercolor Resist

Crayons and oil pastels show through.

More About...
Technique Tips

Collage

Using Scissors

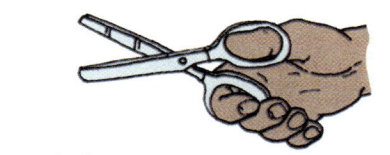

Hold scissors this way.

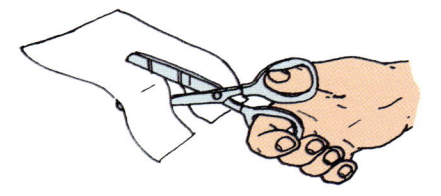

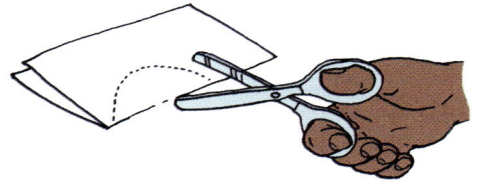

Always cut away from your body.

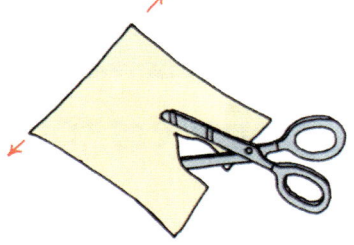

Have a friend stretch cloth as you cut.

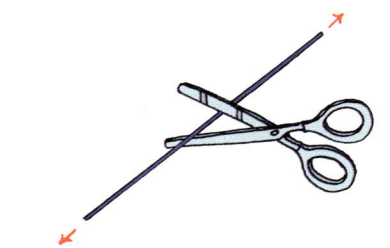

Do the same with yarn.

More About...
Technique Tips

Using Glue

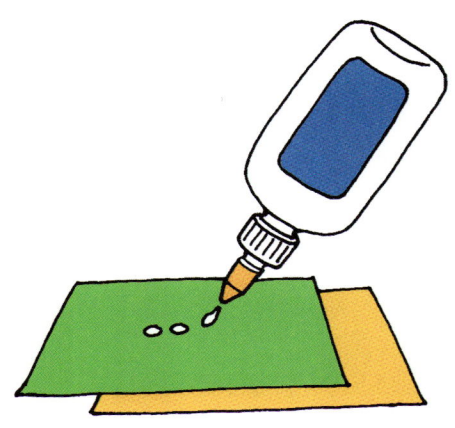

Use only a few glue dots on one paper.
Smooth with the tip of the glue bottle.

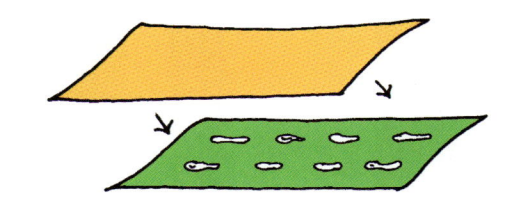

Press the papers together.

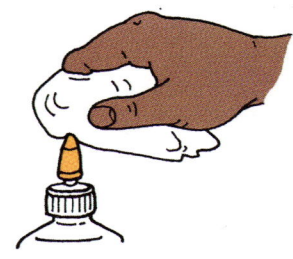

Clean the top and close the bottle.

More About...
Technique Tips

Arranging a Design

Tear shapes.

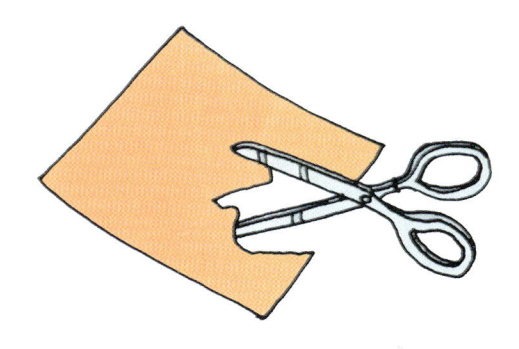

Cut shapes.

Use real objects.

1. Make a design.

   Do you like the shapes and spaces?
   Do you like the colors?
   Do you like the textures?

2. Glue the pieces into place.

More About... Technique Tips

Printmaking

Making a Stamp Print

Paint the stamp.

Press the stamp onto paper and lift.

More About... Technique Tips

Sculpting

Working with Clay

Squeeze, pull, and shape to make clay soft.

Squeeze and pinch.

Pinch and pull.

Carving Clay

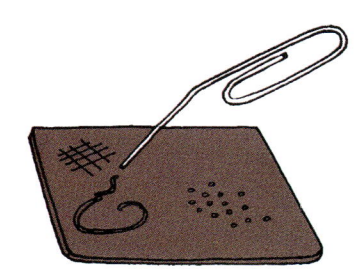

Use a pointed tool.

More About... Technique Tips

Embroidery

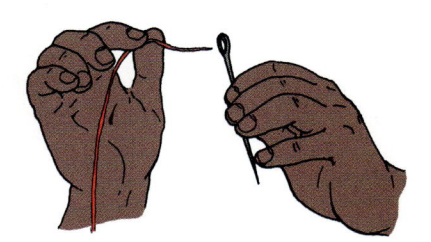

Thread a needle.

Use a running stitch.

More About... Technique Tips

Weaving

Making a Paper Loom

1. Fold paper in half.

2. Cut on folded edge.

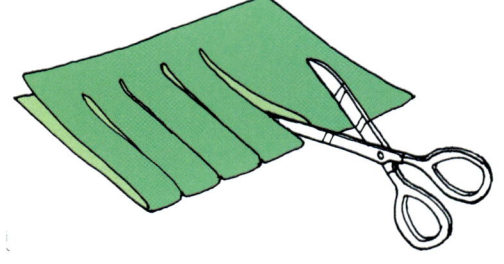

3. Don't cut to the other end.

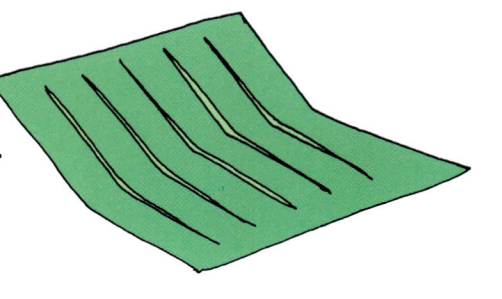

Weaving on a Paper Loom

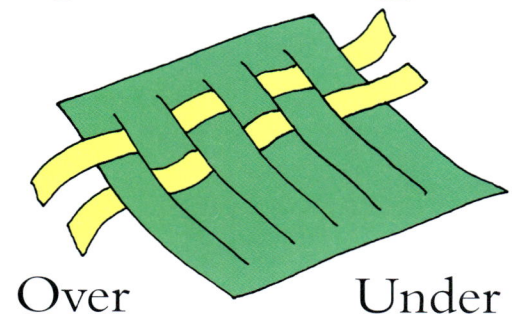

Over   Under

More About...
Art Criticism

Grant Wood. (American). *American Gothic.* 1930. Oil on beaverboard. 74.3 × 62.4 cm. The Art Institute of Chicago, Illinois. © 1998 Estate of Grant Wood/Licensed by VAGA, New York, NY.

More About... Art Criticism

DESCRIBE

Who do you see?

What do you see?

ANALYZE

What colors do you see?

What shapes do you see?

More About...
Art Criticism

Grant Wood. (American). *American Gothic.* 1930. Oil on beaverboard. 74.3 × 62.4 cm. The Art Institute of Chicago, Illinois. © 1998 Estate of Grant Wood/Licensed by VAGA, New York, NY.

More About... Art Criticism

INTERPRET

What is happening in the painting?

DECIDE

Have you seen other artworks like this?

More About... Aesthetics

LOOK

Look at the painting.

Grant Wood. (American). *American Gothic.* 1930. Oil on beaverboard. 74.3 × 62.4 cm. The Art Institute of Chicago, Illinois. © 1998 Estate of Grant Wood/Licensed by VAGA, New York, NY.

More About... Aesthetics

LOOK AGAIN

Look at the painting.

What do you hear?

What do you think is in the house?

More About... Aesthetics

LOOK INSIDE

Look at the painting.

Pretend you are in the work of art.

What are you doing?

Grant Wood. (American). *American Gothic.* 1930. Oil on beaverboard. 74.3 × 62.4 cm. The Art Institute of Chicago, Illinois. © 1998 Estate of Grant Wood/Licensed by VAGA, New York, NY.

More About... Aesthetics

LOOK OUTSIDE

Look at the painting.

What are the people thinking?

What do the people see?

What will you remember about this work?

More About...
Art History

Artist unknown.
Yellow Horse. (Chinese Horse).
15,000–10,000 B.C. France.

140

Artist unknown.
Tutankhamen Mask (side view).
c. 1340 B.C. Egypt.

More About...Art History

More About...
Art History

Leonardo da Vinci.
Mona Lisa. 1503. Italy.

Mary Cassatt.
Susan Comforting the Baby. 1881.
United States.

More About…Art History

More About...
Subject Matter

Artists make art about many subjects. What subjects do you see here?

People

Mary Cassatt. (American). *Spring: Margot Standing in a Garden.* 1902. Oil on canvas. $26\frac{3}{4} \times 22\frac{3}{4}$ inches. The Metropolitan Museum of Art, NY. Bequest of Ruth Alms Barnard (1982.119.2).

More About...
Subject Matter

Objects

Vincent van Gogh. (Dutch). *Irises.* c. 1880. Oil on canvas. 29 × 36$\frac{1}{4}$ inches. Metropolitan Museum of Art, New York. Gift of Adele R. Levy, 1958. Photograph by Malcom Varon.

Stories

Edward Hicks. (American). *Noah's Ark.* 1846. Oil on canvas. 26$\frac{5}{16}$ × 30$\frac{3}{8}$ inches. Philadelphia Museum of Art: Bequest of Lisa Norris Elkins.

More About...
Subject Matter

Things Outside

Currier and Ives. (American). *A Ride to School.* Nineteenth century. Color lithograph. 5 × 8 inches. The Metropolitan Museum of Art, New York, NY.

Colors and Shapes

Joan Miró. (Spanish). *Woman and Bird in the Moonlight.* 1949. The Tate Gallery, London, England. ©1998 Artists Rights Society (ARS), New York/ADAGP, Paris.

More About...
Subject Matter

Everyday Life

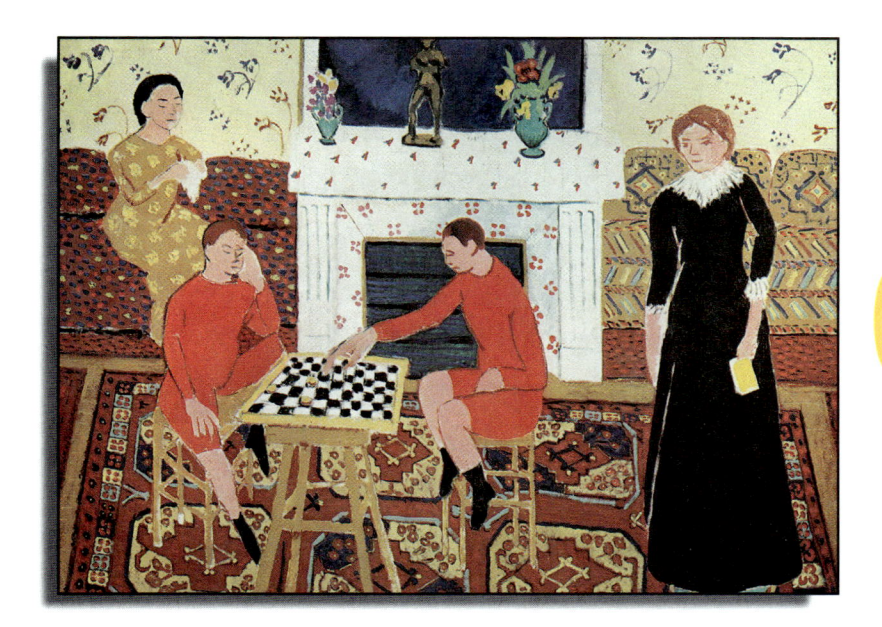

Henri Matisse. (French). *The Family of the Painter.* 1911. The Hermitage Museum, St. Petersburg, Russia. Scala, Art Resource, NY. ©1998 Artists Rights Society (ARS), NY.

Things with a Deeper Meaning

Bookcover: Mary Emmerling's American Country Hearts. Photograph by Chris Mead. ©1988 by Chris Mead, Inc. Reprinted by permission of Clarkson N. Potter, a division of Crown Publishers, Inc.

More About...Subject Matter 147

More About...
Seeing Lines

Most pictures have lines you already know.

More About... Seeing Lines

LOOK

Find these lines in the picture.

Straight

Curved

Zigzag

More About...
Seeing Shapes

Most pictures have shapes you already know.

150 More About...Seeing Shapes

More About...
Seeing Shapes

LOOK

Look for these shapes in the picture.

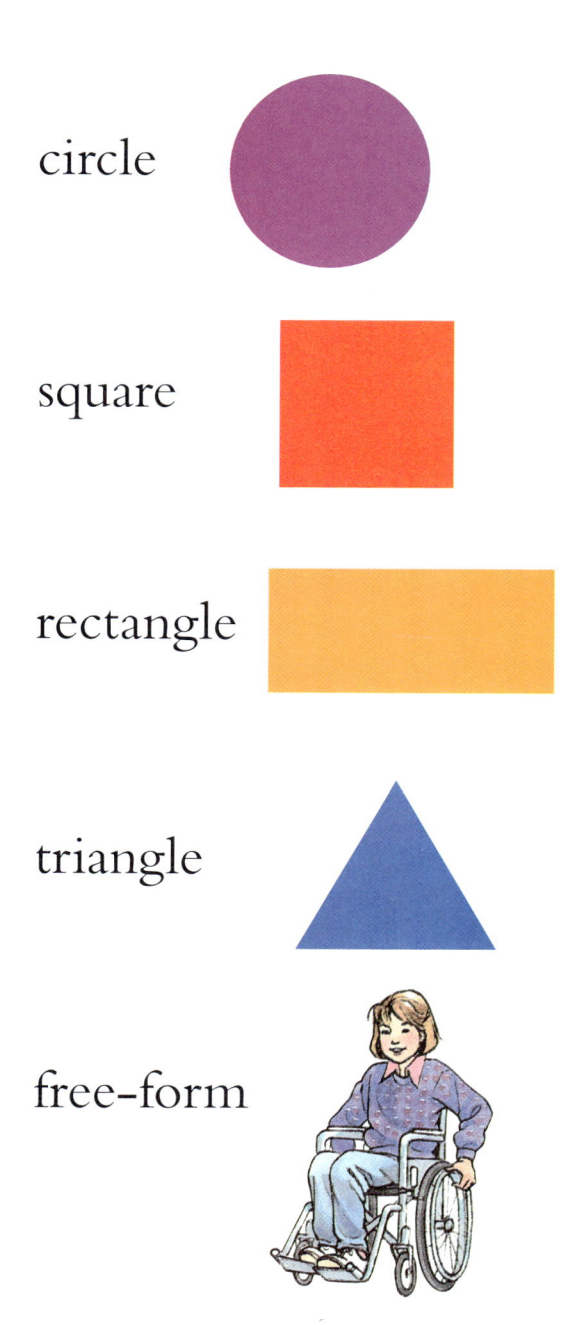

circle

square

rectangle

triangle

free-form

More About...Seeing Shapes   151

More About...
Seeing Size

What makes things look large or small?

More About...
Seeing Size

LOOK

Look at the picture.

Which horse is largest?

Which horse is smaller?

Which horse is smallest?

Visual Index: Artworks Arranged in Time Order

Artist unknown
Painted Storage Jar
2500–1700 B.C.
page 78

Artist unknown
Ancient Egyptian Hippo "William"
1991–1786 B.C.
page 74

Artist unknown
Ravenna Apse Mosaic (detail)
A.D. 549
page 22

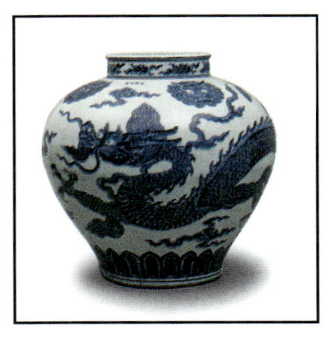

Artist unknown
Jar
1426–1435
page 58

Katsushika Hokusai
Boy Juggling Shells
Edo period
page 20

Ralph Earl
Mrs. Noah Smith and Her Family
c. 1780
page 42

154 Visual Index

Visual Index

Itō Jakuchū
Fukurojin, the God of Longevity and Wisdom
1790
page 18

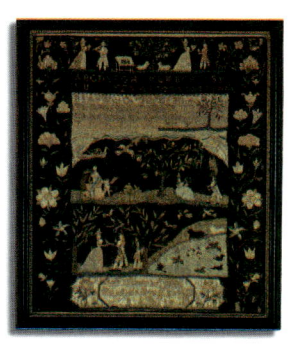

Patty Coggeshall
Sampler
c. 1792
page 96

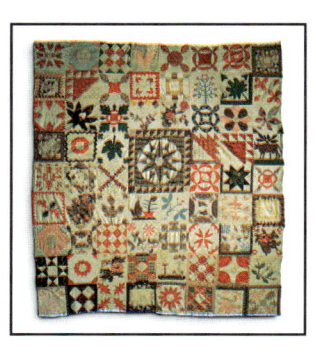

Artist unknown
Album Quilt
1841–1844
page 34

Winslow Homer
Snap the Whip
1872
page 24

Artist unknown
Classic Serape Style Wearing Blanket
1875
page 14

W.H. Brown
Bareback Riders
1886
page 16

Visual Index 155

Visual Index

Artist unknown
Hand Puppets
Late nineteenth century
page 90

Artist unknown
Fish, Gold Weight
Nineteenth-twentieth century
page 94

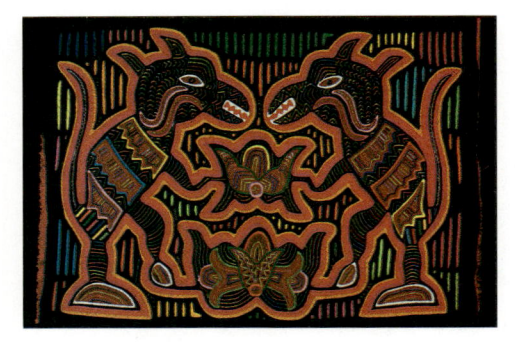

Artist unknown
Mola
Twentieth century
page 108

Felipa Trujillo
Man
Early 1900s
page 70

Gabriele Münter
Child with Ball
c. 1916
page 88

Allan Rohan Crite
School's Out
1936
page 38

Visual Index

William H. Johnson
Li'l Sis
1944
page 40

Artist unknown
Butterfly
c. 1950
page 106

Artist unknown
Szopka
c. 1960
page 72

Claes Oldenburg
Two Cheeseburgers With Everything (Dual Hamburgers)
1962
page 52

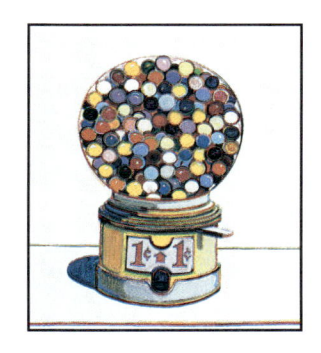

Wayne Thiebaud
Jawbreaker Machine
1963
page 54

Artist unknown
Bottle Cap Giraffe
1966
page 76

Visual Index 157

Visual Index

Jack Savitsky
Train in Coal Town
1968
page 110

Betty Parsons
Winged Frog
1978
page 86

Dorothea Rockburne
Sheba
1980
page 68

Kenny Scharf
When Worlds Collide
1984
page 32

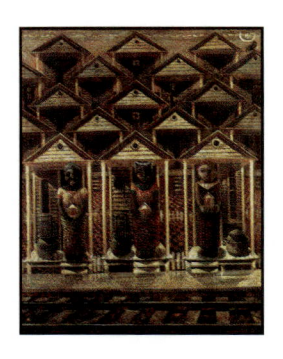

John Biggers
Shotguns, Fourth Ward
1987
page 114

Chuck Close
Self Portrait
1987
page 104

Visual Index

David Wiesner
Free Fall
1988
page 36

Artist unknown
Appalachian Basket
1988
page 92

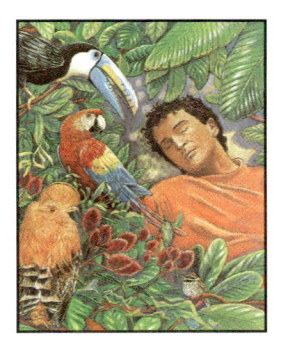

Lynne Cherry
The Great Kapok Tree
1990
page 56

Graeme Base
Act II, Scene I "The Deep"
1992
page 60

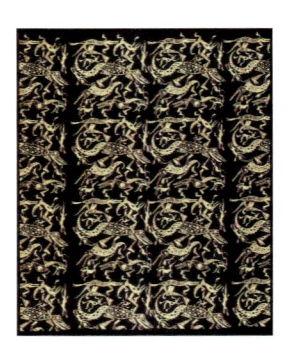

Artist unknown
Printed Fabric from Bambalulu
1993
page 112

Peggy Flora Zalucha
Sprinkler Garden
1994
page 50

Visual Index 159

Glossary

art form

A type of art.

black

blue

bright color

broken line

brown

circle

collage

Bits and pieces of things glued onto paper.

curved line

darker

Glossary

dull color

geometric shapes

even balance

Both halves are equal. Left side and right side are the same.

fiber

A material used to make baskets and cloth. Grass, yarn, and straw are kinds of fibers.

green

form

lighter

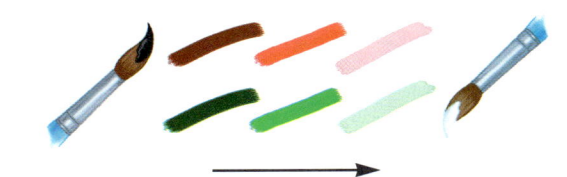

free-form shape

line

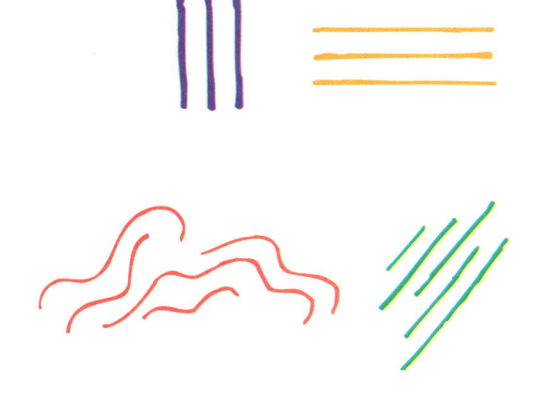

Glossary 161

Glossary

movement

printing

Pressing a shape from one thing to another many times.

mural

A painting done on a wall.

purple

orange

real texture

Texture you can feel.

outline

rectangle

red

painting

An art form using paint on a flat surface.

162

Glossary

Glossary

rhythm

shape

rough line

slanted line

sculpture

A kind of art form that can be seen from all sides.

smooth line

Glossary 163

Glossary

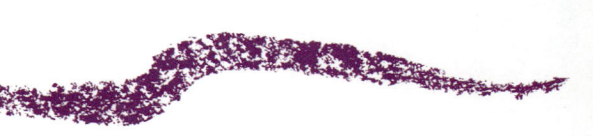

space

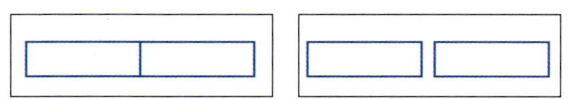

texture
How something feels.

square

thick line

stitchery
Art made with yarn on cloth.

thin line

straight line

triangle

Glossary

Glossary

unity

A feeling of belonging together.

visual rhythm

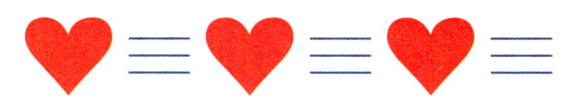

visual texture

Texture you can see, but cannot touch.

white

yellow

Index

A
Act II, Scene 1 "The Deep," 60
Album Quilt, 34
Ancient Egyptian Hippo "William," 74
animals, 74-75, 76-77, 106-107, 112-113
Appalachian Basket, 92
art forms, 79

B
balance, 104-107
Bareback Riders, 16
Base, Graeme, 60
Biggers, John, 114
black, 51
blue, 51, 60
Bottle Cap Giraffe, 76
Boy Juggling Shells, 20
bright colors, 56-59
broken lines, 22-23
brown, 51
Brown, W. H., 16
buildings, 72-73
Butterfly, 106

C
Cherry, Lynne, 56
Child with Ball, 88
circle, 34-35
Classic Serape Style Wearing Blanket, 14
Close, Chuck, 104

Coggeshall, Patty, 96
collage, 53, 55, 87
colors, 50-61, 108-109, 115
Crite, Allan Rohan, 38
curved lines, 16-17

D
dark colors, 60-61
darker, 61
dull colors, 56-59

E
Earl, Ralph, 42
embroidery, 96-97
empty areas, 68-69
even balance, 105-107

F
feelings, 58-59
fibers, 91, 92-93
Fish, Gold Weight, 94
forms, 70-79, 94
Free Fall, 36
free-form shapes, 36-41
Fukurojin, the God of Longevity and Wisdom, 18

G
geometric shapes, 34-35, 38-40
The Great Kapok Tree, 56
green, 51

Index

H
Hand Puppets, 90
Hokusai, Katsushika, 20
Homer, Winslow, 24

J
Jakuchū, Itō, 18
Jar (Ming dynasty), 58
Jawbreaker Machine, 54
Johnson, William H., 40

L
light colors, 60-61
lighter, 61
lines, 14-19, 20-25, 108-109
Li'l Sis, 40

M
Man, 70
Mola, 108
movement, 110-111
moving lines, 24-25
Mrs. Noah Smith and Her Family, 42
Münter, Gabriele, 88
mural, 115

N
narrow, 15

O
Oldenburg, Claes, 52
orange, 51
outline, 32-33

P
Painted Storage Jar, 78
Parsons, Betty, 86
patterns, 108
Printed Fabric, 112
printing, 36-37, 112-113
purple, 51

R
Ravenna Apse Mosaic (Detail), 22
real texture, 87, 95, 97
rectangle, 34-35
red, 51-52
rhythm, 108-109, 110-111
Rockburne, Dorothea, 68
rough, 18, 86
rough lines, 18-19

S
Sampler, 96
Savitsky, Jack, 110
Scharf, Kenny, 32
School's Out, 38
sculpture, 70-71, 74-75
Self Portrait, 104
shapes, 32-33, 36-39, 43-44, 57, 68-69, 96, 105, 108-110, 112-115
Sheba, 68
Shotguns, Fourth Ward, 114
sight, 88
slanted lines, 16-17
smooth lines, 18-19
Snap the Whip, 24

Index

solid forms, 73, 75
solid shape, 71
space, 68-69
Sprinkler Garden, 50
square, 34-35
straight lines, 16-17
Szopka, 72

T

Technique Tips, 120-131
  collage, 125-127
    arranging a design, 127
    using glue, 126
    using scissors, 125
  drawing, 120-121
    colored chalk, 121
    crayon, 120
    marker, 120
    oil pastels, 121
    pencil, 120
  embroidery, 130
  painting, 122-124
    taking care of your paintbrush, 122
    tempera, 123
    watercolor, 124
    watercolor resist, 124
  printmaking, 128
    making a stamp print, 128
  sculpting, 129
    carving clay, 129
    working with clay, 129
  weaving, 131
    making a paper loom, 131
    weaving on a paper loom, 131

texture, 86-97
  real texture, 87, 95, 97
  visual texture, 89
thick lines, 14-15
Thiebaud, Wayne, 54
thin lines, 14-15
touch, 20-21, 86-88, 92, 94
Train in Coal Town, 110
triangle, 34-35
Trujillo, Felipa, 70
Two Cheeseburgers With Everything, 52

U

unity, 114-115

V

visual rhythm, 109
visual texture, 89

W

weaving, 92-93
When Worlds Collide, 32
white, 51
wide, 15
Wiesner, David, 36
Winged Frog, 86

Y

yellow, 51

Z

Zalucha, Peggy Flora, 50

Florida Art Connections

The artworks on these pages are connected to Florida. You can use them to learn more about Florida. You can also use them to practice writing.

Follow the directions on each page. Then ask yourself the questions on page FL8.

FLORIDA WRITES! Practice

Florida Art Connections
Expository Writing Practice

Anna Vaughn Hyatt Huntington. (American). *Yawning Panther*. Bronze. $5 \frac{1}{2} \times 14 \frac{3}{4} \times 5 \frac{1}{4}$ inches. The National Museum of Women in the Arts, Washington, DC. Gift of Wallace and Wilhelmina Holladay.

Think About It

This is a sculpture of a panther. Some panthers live in Florida. Florida Panthers are wild animals with soft, brown fur.

Tell About It

Does this panther look real? Tell why you think it looks real. Then draw a picture of it.

Florida Art Connections
Expository Writing Practice

Jane Peterson. (American). *Beach Scene.* Oil on canvasboard. 12 × 15 7/8 inches. The National Museum of Women in the Arts, Washington, DC. Gift of Caryl and Martin Horowitz.

Think About It

Florida has many beaches. Does this look like a beach you have seen?

Tell About It

Tell about the colors you see at the beach. Use those colors to draw a picture of a beach.

Florida Art Connections
Expository Writing Practice

Carmen Lomas Garza. (American). *Naranjas (Oranges)*. Gouache. 20 × 14 inches. Collection of Mr. and Mrs. Ira Schneider, Scottsdale, Arizona. Photo by Wolfgang Dietze.

Think About It

This picture shows a family. They are picking oranges. There are many orange trees in Florida. You can make many different foods with oranges.

Tell About It

Name some foods made with oranges. Draw a picture of a food made with oranges.

FL4 FLORIDA WRITES! Practice

Florida Art Connections
Narrative Writing Practice

Anna Vaughn Hyatt Huntington. (American). *Yawning Panther*. Bronze. $5\frac{1}{2} \times 14\frac{3}{4} \times 5\frac{1}{4}$ inches. The National Museum of Women in the Arts, Washington, DC. Gift of Wallace and Wilhelmina Holladay.

Think About It

This panther looks like it is resting. In Florida, panthers sleep in trees. Where do you sleep?

Tell About It

Pretend you are a panther. Tell a story about taking a nap in a tree. Then draw a picture of a panther in a tree.

Florida Art Connections
Narrative Writing Practice

Jane Peterson. (American). *Beach Scene*. Oil on canvasboard. 12 × 15 $\frac{7}{8}$ inches. The National Museum of Women in the Arts, Washington, DC. Gift of Caryl and Martin Horowitz.

Think About It

What are the people in the painting doing?
What do people do at beaches in Florida?

Tell About It

Tell a story about a day at the beach.
Then draw a picture of your story.

FLORIDA WRITES! Practice

Florida Art Connections
Narrative Writing Practice

Carmen Lomas Garza. (American). *Naranjas (Oranges)*. Gouache. 20 × 14 inches. Collection of Mr. and Mrs. Ira Schneider, Scottsdale, Arizona. Photo by Wolfgang Dietze.

Think About It

Oranges need warm weather to grow. Florida is a good place for oranges to grow. When the oranges are ripe, they have to be picked. Pretend you are helping this family pick oranges.

Tell About It

What could you do to help this family? Draw a picture of yourself picking oranges.

FLORIDA WRITES! Practice

Florida Art Connections
Self-Assessment

Ask these questions after each lesson. If you answer no to any question, go back and check your work. Make changes if you need to.

1. Did I follow the directions?
2. Did I draw a complete picture?
3. Did I include everything?
4. Can others understand my drawing?